Bible reflections
for older people

BRF

The Bible Reading Fellowship
15 The Chambers, Vineyard
Abingdon OX14 3FE
brf.org.uk

The Bible Reading Fellowship (BRF) is a Registered Charity (233280)

ISBN 978 0 85746 910 6
All rights reserved

This edition © The Bible Reading Fellowship 2020
Cover image © iStock/MMPhotography

Acknowledgements

Scripture quotations marked with the following acronyms are taken from the version shown. Where no acronym is given, the quotation is taken from the same version as the headline reference. **NRSV**: The New Revised Standard Version of the Bible, Anglicised edition, copyright © 1989, 1995 by the Division of Christian Education of the National Council of the Churches of Christ in the United States of America. Used by permission. All rights reserved. **NIV**: The Holy Bible, New International Version (Anglicised edition) copyright © 1979, 1984, 2011 by Biblica. Used by permission of Hodder & Stoughton Publishers, a Hachette UK company. All rights reserved. 'NIV' is a registered trademark of Biblica. UK trademark number 1448790. **CEV**: The Contemporary English Version. New Testament © American Bible Society 1991, 1992, 1995. Old Testament © American Bible Society 1995. Anglicisations © British & Foreign Bible Society 1996. Used by permission. **GW**: God's Word Translation Copyright © 1995 by God's Word to the Nations. Used by permission of God's Word Mission Society. **NLT**: The Holy Bible, New Living Translation, copyright © 1996, 2004, 2007, 2013. Used by permission of Tyndale House Publishers, Inc., Carol Stream, Illinois 60188. All rights reserved. **KJV**: The Authorised Version of the Bible (The King James Bible), the rights in which are vested in the Crown, are reproduced by permission of the Crown's Patentee, Cambridge University Press.

Every effort has been made to trace and contact copyright owners for material used in this resource. We apologise for any inadvertent omissions or errors, and would ask those concerned to contact us so that full acknowledgement can be made in the future.

A catalogue record for this book is available from the British Library

Printed and bound in the UK by Zenith Media NP4 0DQ

Contents

About the writers

Heather Pencavel is a retired minister in the United Reformed Church. She worked in industrial chaplaincy in Bristol and later edited the national monthly magazine of the Industrial Mission Association. Heather's passion is writing, and she has written poems, prayers and reflections for various anthologies.

Emlyn Williams worked for many years for Scripture Union, latterly for SU International, and spent much of his time with Christians in eastern Europe. He is a writer of many individual and group Bible materials and is currently discipleship pastor working as part of the leadership team in a large Anglican church.

David Butterfield was successful in the 2017 writing competition for readers of *The Upper Room* Bible reading notes. After studying music he felt the call to ordination in the Church of England. During his 40-year ministry he served at churches in Southport, the Midlands and Shropshire. His final post was based at York Minster, from which he retired in 2017.

Angela Tilby worked for the BBC as a producer of religious programmes for 22 years. Ordained in 1997, she became a tutor at Westcott House in Cambridge. After some years as a parish priest she moved to Oxford as diocesan canon of Christ Church Cathedral. She writes for the *Church Times*, broadcasts frequently on Radio 4's *Thought for the Day* and is a canon emeritus of Christ Church Cathedral.

From the Editor

Welcome to this new collection of Bible reflections.

As a child with waist-length blonde hair I was regularly cast as the angel Gabriel in school nativity plays. 'Fear not!' I bellowed at inky-fingered shepherds in dressing gowns and Clarks sandals. A tinsel halo and tinfoil wings completed my costume.

Angels have a significant role in Judaism, Christianity and Islam: they exist to praise God, to interact with human beings and to serve as God's messengers and agents in the world. Their popularity has waxed and waned down the centuries but has been notably high in recent years, even in the wider, secular world.

From blindingly bright, awe-inspiring – even terrifying – figures to comforting companions and protectors, these divine envoys have a unique hold on our imaginations and have featured prominently in Christian art and iconography through the ages.

This issue of *Bible Reflections for Older People* covers Advent and Christmas, and angels feature prominently here too: from Angela Tilby's thoughtful series, 'God's messengers', through Denise Line's charming description of an abbey's 'Angel project', to the words of a much-loved Victorian hymn and a reimagining of the angels' message to 21st-century 'shepherds'.

So, with Denise and Angela and all our other contributors, I wish you the joy of the angels.

God bless you.

Using these reflections

Perhaps you have always had a special daily time for reading the Bible and praying. But now, as you grow older, you are finding it more difficult to keep to a regular pattern or find it hard to concentrate. Or maybe you've never done this before. Whatever your situation, these Bible reflections aim to help you take a few moments to read God's word and pray, whenever you have time or feel that would be helpful.

When to read them

You may find it helpful to use these Bible reflections in the morning or last thing at night, or any time during the day. There are 40 daily reflections here, grouped around four themes. Each one includes some verses from the Bible, a reflection to help you in your own thinking about God, and a prayer suggestion. The reflections aren't dated, so it doesn't matter if you don't want to read every day. The Bible verses are printed, but if you'd like to read from your own Bible that's fine too.

How to read them

- **Take time** to quieten yourself, becoming aware of God's presence, asking him to speak to you through the Bible and the reflection.

- **Read** the Bible verses and the reflection:
  - What do you especially like or find helpful in these verses?
  - What might God be saying to you through this reading?
  - Is there something to pray about or thank God for?

- **Pray**. Each reflection includes a prayer suggestion. You might like to pray for yourself or take the opportunity to think about and pray for others.

Let us go singing

Heather Pencavel

Singing, I believe, is built into human DNA. If you are thinking, 'Not mine!' – think again. If, like me, you were discouraged from singing as a child or told you were tone deaf, don't worry; you probably aren't. Tone deafness affects only 4% of the population.

Singing is built into the DNA of the universe too. In 2017 astronomers in Birmingham discovered that a cluster of stars, 13 billion years old, buried within our galaxy, was 'singing'. Stars make sound naturally and this gets trapped, like sound in a musical instrument. As the star resonates, because of the sound trapped inside, it 'breathes' in and out, which makes it appear brighter as it heats up and get dimmer as it cools down.

The writer of Job got it right about the creation of the universe: 'when the morning stars sang together' (Job 38:7, NRSV).

The Bible tells many stories of the power of song to inspire, to comfort, to remember past times and eternal truth, to express joy or sorrow, to change lives and to celebrate the beauty of creation. Let us go singing!

Exodus 15:20–21a (NRSV)

Miriam's song

Then the prophet Miriam, Aaron's sister, took a tambourine in her hand; and all the women went out after her with tambourines and with dancing. And Miriam sang to them: 'Sing to the Lord, for he has triumphed gloriously.'

The first song in the Bible was sung by women – scholars note that the song of Moses (Exodus 15:1–18) was added centuries later, after exile in Babylon. The story of the exodus is a foundation stone of Jewish faith. Practising Jews still read it every week.

Miriam's song is a spontaneous, heartfelt expression of praise to God for release. The women danced and sang and beat out the rhythm on their tambourines – while the bodies of Egyptian horsemen sank in the Red Sea as the waters receded. This was not just victory – it was freedom.

Today we might feel more like singing a lament at our world's conflicts and divisions, the dying forests and the rising waters; our human failure to care for the earth and its people. There are still people in the UK who are enslaved and longing to see their home again.

I belong to a community choir. Our concerts raise money for local charities. Next time, perhaps, we'll sing for an environment group or an anti-slavery charity.

■ PRAYER

Loving God, we thank you: you made the stars to sing; you give us the gift of song and plenty to sing about. Give us courage to lift our voices in songs of thanksgiving and of penitence. Amen

2 Samuel 18:33 (NRSV)

A song of sorrow

The king [David] was deeply moved… and wept; and as he went, he said, 'O my son Absalom, my son, my son Absalom! Would that I had died instead of you, O Absalom, my son, my son!'

'It should have been me,' David cried, as bereaved parents often do. His tears and his heartbreaking song for Absalom look like the triumph of sentiment over sense. Love often does.

Absalom was a rebel: his death was the result of his attempt to take the kingdom from his father. Yet David still loved his wayward son with a father's love. That is how God loves us – not because of what we do, but because of what we are: God's beloved.

When someone we love dies, we don't usually feel like singing. But we do sing – we choose funeral music and suitable hymns and songs, involving family members in the process. Remembering and celebrating the person who has died can bring comfort in sadness. We find that we can express, in song and in tears, deep feelings for which we could not find our own words. Often this is the beginning of healing for our sorrow and loss – and anger, if that is what we feel. Singing together, even a lament, can soothe our sorrow and heal our pain.

■ **PRAYER**

God of all comfort, when we sing through our tears, embrace us with your love. Amen

Ecclesiastes 3:1–4, 12 (NRSV, abridged)

A song of contentment

For everything there is a season... a time to be born, and a time to die... a time to weep, and a time to laugh; a time to mourn, and a time to dance... There is nothing better for [people] than to be happy and enjoy themselves as long as they live.

Looking for texts in the Bible about singing, and finding songs about the highs and lows of life, I realised that I sing most when I am content: not feeling low, not on a high – just content. This is a song of contentment.

It is often read at funerals, so we associate it with death. It's actually a poem about life: its rich variety and its human ordinariness. Birth and death, planting and gathering, tears and laughter, mourning and dancing – contentment.

We do not know what each day will be like until we live it, nor do we know what tomorrow will bring. We know we've been born, we will die and in between are laughter and tears, joy and sadness, love and loss, company and solitude, work and idleness. There is a time for everything. In the meantime there is order in life: day and night, the cycle of the seasons, pleasure in living, faith in God's future – contentment.

■ **PRAYER**

God of peace and love, teach us wherever we are, whatever we do, whatever happens, to trust you and be content. Amen

Song of Songs 2:8, 10–12a (NRSV)

A song of love and creation

The voice of my beloved! Look, he comes, leaping upon the mountains, bounding over the hills... My beloved speaks and says to me: 'Arise, my love, my fair one, and come away; for now the winter is past, the rain is over and gone. The flowers appear on the earth; the time of singing has come.'

This poem fizzes and sparkles with the joy of spring and with delight in the created world and in human love. The lover leaps on the mountains, in harmony with the earth. Spring has come, flowers blossom and birds are singing – a perfect setting for love. All creation is in unity: as it was meant to be; as it no longer is. This is the kind of world we would like to pass on to future generations. But the land has been defiled, forests destroyed and rivers and seas polluted by tons of plastic.

This generation of young people, led by a teenager called Greta, has inspired thousands of people to action, highlighting the slow destruction of the earth resulting from human activity. God's earth is ours to care for. This ancient poem celebrates the harmony that we have lost. Our church is working towards becoming an eco-church – using every means possible to reduce our use of energy (except the human sort!). Is your church involved? Could it be?

■ **PRAYER**
Creating God, for the beautiful earth, for human love, we give you thanks. For the spoiling of the earth and for love rejected, we ask forgiveness. Amen

Psalm 137:1, 3–4 (NRSV)

A song of exile

By the rivers of Babylon – there we sat down and there we wept when we remembered Zion... For there our captors asked us for songs, and our tormentors asked for mirth, saying, 'Sing us one of the songs of Zion!' How could we sing the Lord's song in a foreign land?

The songs we know from childhood often stay with us. I remember choruses sung at Sunday school and songs we learnt at school. The songs I remember most are the songs my father used to sing. He served in World War I and spent some years as a prisoner of war in Germany. When I was very young, the sound of 'Keep the home fires burning' or 'It's a long way to Tipperary' would signal that Daddy was home from work.

'Did you sing that song when you were in the camp, Daddy?' I asked once, probably imagining a kind of Brownie camp for men. 'No!' he shouted. 'It wasn't for the Germans!' And the door slammed behind him.

'How could we sing the Lord's song in a foreign land?' the former exiles cried. 'They want to laugh at us as they did when they tore down our holy temple.' Some wounds go deep. And some evil deeds need to be remembered – so that they may never happen again.

■ **PRAYER**

God of love and justice, when we are mocked or belittled, show us how to forgive and what it is necessary to forget, so that change may come peaceably. Amen

Psalm 96:1–2, 10a, 13b (NRSV)

A song of truth and justice

O sing to the Lord a new song; sing to the Lord, all the earth. Sing to the Lord, bless his name; tell of his salvation from day to day... Say among the nations, 'The Lord is king!...' He will judge the world with righteousness, and the peoples with his truth.

The last two lines of this quotation leap out at me. Just now righteousness – justice – and truth do not seem much in fashion. When people in power deny the truth and promote whatever story will fit in with their scheming, and when we see the deliberate stirring up of violence and the wanton stoking of division, we are not seeing God's reign of peace based on justice and truth. It makes me feel angry and sad – and helpless... until I read the first two lines of this psalm.

'Sing to the Lord a new song' – a song people don't yet know; a song about salvation and justice and truth; a song of hope for us to sing, for we too need to hear it, among the clamour of the world. We sing it as we continue to be faithful witnesses to God's love and truth and justice; as we make people welcome, support them and encourage conversation. With or without words, we 'tell of his salvation from day to day'.

■ PRAYER

Ever-faithful God, in the clamour help us to listen for your song of salvation and hope, and teach us to sing. Amen

Luke 1:49, 52–53 (NRSV)

A song of justice and joy

'For the Mighty One has done great things for me, and holy is his name... He has brought down the powerful from their thrones, and lifted up the lowly; He has filled the hungry with good things, and sent the rich away empty.'

Pregnant teenagers and childless women are unremarkable in our society. In Mary's day, both were ostracised. Elizabeth lived through many years of private sadness and public shame because she was childless. Now in old age, she is pregnant. Mary is young, unmarried and also pregnant. She faces disgrace in her community, so she goes to the hill country to her cousin.

She might have feared rejection from the older woman; instead, she finds welcome.

Mary's joyful song rings through the house. *Magnificat* – God is great – the Saviour, the Mighty One, who chooses ordinary, lowly people and blesses them with justice. Now, in Mary's child, through Mary's obedience, God will raise up one who will rescue the oppressed and bring God's truth and justice and everlasting love to all people – as Jesus did, starting with a dozen or so working men and women in Galilee and continuing in the lives of ordinary people who have done extraordinary things for over two thousand years.

God keeps faith 'according to the promise he made to our ancestors, to Abraham and to his descendants forever' (Luke 1:55).

■ PRAYER

Thank you, God of grace, that you keep your promises, not just for a while but forever. Amen

Mark 14:26–27 (NRSV)

Singing together

When they had sung the hymn, they went out to the Mount of Olives. And Jesus said to them, 'You will all become deserters; for it is written, "I will strike the shepherd, and the sheep will be scattered."'

I wonder what the hymn was at the end of the Passover meal. The disciples had just experienced the strangest Passover of their lives. Passover is usually celebrated at home, as a family meal, but here they all were in a stranger's house in Jerusalem, without their families. That must have felt wrong.

Passover is a joyful ceremony, celebrating the exodus of the people of Israel from slavery in Egypt. Here the atmosphere was sombre. Jesus told his friends that he was expecting betrayal by one of them. Each one suspected everyone, including himself – 'Is it I?'; 'It's one of you.' Then came the ritual of the bread and wine, which Jesus called his body and blood. What did he mean?

How did they feel as they sang that last hymn – traditionally a song of praise? Singing brings people together as their voices blend. I think Jesus spoke very gently when he said, 'You will all desert me… but we'll meet again in Galilee. I will lead you.'

Jesus says to all of us, when we need to hear it: 'We'll meet again… I will lead you.'

■ PRAYER

God of comfort and strength, when it is hard to sing, teach us your songs of love and hold us fast. Amen

Acts 16:24–26 (NRSV, abridged)

Singing in the dark

[The jailer] put [Paul and Silas] in the innermost cell and fastened their feet in the stocks. About midnight Paul and Silas were praying and singing hymns to God, and the prisoners were listening to them. Suddenly there was an earthquake… and everyone's chains were unfastened.

It was late December, dark and very cold in the bus station. I waited in a grubby bus for the driver, delayed by Christmas traffic or more serious events – streets blocked by rubble from explosions, or route deviations, police precautions against rioting. This was Belfast in the early 1970s. The bus station was a target for terrorists, as was a nearby hotel.

There were four of us – a young father, his two small sons and me. We sat in silence, most unusual for Ulster folk, who like a good chat with friend or stranger. We were all afraid.

The father put his arms round his boys and drew them closer. They leaned into his warmth. Slowly and quietly all three began to sing – in Latin, so they were Catholics. A risky statement: *Adeste fideles, Laeti triumphantes, Venite, venite in Bethlehem…*

'O come, all ye faithful' – I sang along with them and, as we sang, the fear left us. No earthquake – but the chains of fear that held us were unfastened. We travelled home in peace and friendship.

■ PRAYER
Light of the world, when we are afraid, give us courage to sing in the dark. Amen

Revelation 19:6–7a (NRSV)

A song of victory

Then I heard what seemed to be the voice of a great multitude, like the sound of many waters and like the sound of mighty thunderpeals crying out, 'Hallelujah! For the Lord our God, the Almighty reigns. Let us rejoice and exult and give him the glory.'

The choir I belong to is one of ten community choirs run by the same organisation, dotted around the south-west of England. We rehearse once a week, in the afternoon, most of us in churches. We organise workshops in schools and concerts in local venues, including hospitals and care homes. Money raised goes to local charities.

Once a year all the choirs meet for a Big Sing, usually in a cathedral. Each choir will sing and then we all – there are literally hundreds of us – sing together pieces we have rehearsed separately. That is a beautiful experience. The audience enjoys it too.

No, I'm not going to compare our Big Sing to the voices of the multitude in heaven. That choir celebrates the final coming of the reign of God, the reign of justice and truth which we saw in Psalm 96.

That celebration is not yet. Justice and truth are still to be prayed and worked for. Whatever we can do – voluntary work, writing to councillors or MPs, signing petitions, living more simply – all will help. As we travel, let us go singing!

■ PRAYER

When it seems that peace and justice are long in coming, give us courage to go on singing. Amen

Dawning light

Emlyn Williams

Do you often see the dawn? Or is it something you usually sleep through? Perhaps, like me, you have a memory of a particularly significant dawn. My daughter was born on Easter Day – a long time ago – and I took my wife to the hospital in the early hours. As we drove through the suburbs of Melbourne, Australia, in the rear-view mirror of the car I saw the sun rise over the hills behind. For us this wasn't just the dawning of a new day; it was the dawning of a new life, and our lives have never been the same since.

Dawn is a very powerful symbol in the Bible. It's about light overcoming darkness; it's about a new start; above all, it's a symbol of hope. All of these are important themes, and over the coming days we'll explore some of them. If you can, why not get up early one day to see the sun rise? It will stimulate your imagination as we go through these readings. If dawn is really early in your part of the world, perhaps you could go back to bed afterwards.

Genesis 1:3–5 (NIV)

The dawn of time

And God said, 'Let there be light,' and there was light. God saw that the light was good, and he separated the light from the darkness. God called the light 'day', and the darkness he called 'night'. And there was evening, and there was morning – the first day.

You can't stop the dawn. Like it or not, the sun rises every day without fail. So it's hard to imagine a *first* dawn and a *first* day. The more I think about creation, the more mysterious it becomes and the more questions I have. This first dawn was seen only by God and he declared that the light was good. By separating the light from the darkness, he created day and night.

I usually think of light as that which enables me to see things. When I am in the dark with no light, I stumble and trip. But light is not just about visibility; when God created light, he also created time. Evening and morning made up the first day.

There's a personal challenge in all of this. Our time is not unlimited, and the coming of the dawn is a daily reminder that we will not be here forever. As Moses said, 'Teach us to use wisely all the time we have' (Psalm 90:12, CEV).

■ PRAYER
Lord of time, thank you for another day for me to live. Help me to use it wisely for you and for others. Amen

Lamentations 3:22–24 (NRSV)

New hope

The steadfast love of the Lord never ceases, his mercies never come to an end; they are new every morning; great is your faithfulness. 'The Lord is my portion,' says my soul, 'therefore I will hope in him.'

The dawning of a new day is like the turning of a page. Whatever may have gone before, today brings new possibilities. Yet it is so easy to lose hope and feel trapped by our past. These verses remind us that what really matters is not our faith*less*ness but God's faith*ful*ness.

It's easy too to see the day ahead as a long haul as we try to climb the ladder, wanting to live faithfully for God. But because of what Jesus has done, we can start the day forgiven, at the top of the ladder rather than at the bottom.

A number of years ago in Argentina, the owner of a German shepherd dog called Capitan died. Capitan ran away from home, but a week later he was found guarding the grave of his owner. For the following six years, Capitan went back to the grave every night and slept by the side of his master. What a great example of faithfulness. Yet God's faithfulness is even greater.

If you know the hymn 'Great is thy faithfulness',* you may like to sing it now or listen to a recording.

■ **PRAYER**

Faithful God, help me to respond to your great faithfulness by being faithful to you today. Amen

* 'Great is thy faithfulness', Thomas O. Chisholm (1923)

Psalm 30:4–5 (NIV)

Morning joy?

Sing the praises of the Lord, you his faithful people; praise his holy name. For his anger lasts only a moment, but his favour lasts a lifetime; weeping may stay for the night, but rejoicing comes in the morning.

What a great thought for a sleepless night: 'Rejoicing comes in the morning.' In this psalm David is reflecting on a time of sickness (see verse 2). God had healed him, and the light of morning had overcome the darkness of night. Have you had experiences of darkness being replaced by joy? Take time to recall them and, as the psalm tells us, to praise God.

But I'm tempted to respond to these verses with, 'If only!' Clearly the morning doesn't always resolve our difficulties. The reality is that we all go through times of darkness, times when God may feel distant, times when we may feel that he is angry with us. In such times, it's even more important to recall God's faithfulness in the past.

Perhaps you or someone close to you is experiencing the weeping of the night right now. Pray that their dawn will come quickly. A well-known hymn describes the exchange which God can make as we come to him: 'Mornings of joy give for evenings of tearfulness, trust for our trembling and hope for our fear.'*

■ PRAYER

Lord of the morning, help me to remember today the times when you have exchanged my sadness for joy. Amen

---

* 'O worship the lord in the beauty of holiness', John S.B. Monsell (1863)

Malachi 4:2–3 (NIV)

Healing rays

'But for you who revere my name, the sun of righteousness will rise with healing in its rays. And you will go out and frolic like well-fed calves. Then you will trample on the wicked; they will be ashes under the soles of your feet on the day when I act,' says the Lord Almighty.

If you're anything like me, you probably worry about the state of the world. Why is there such injustice? Why such corruption? Why such illness and pain? And for me, one of the hardest questions is why God *seems* to do nothing about this.

These are not new questions. Around 450 years before Jesus, Malachi wrote about what God would do. God *will act*, he says. A coming day of judgement *will* lead to justice and righteousness. This *will* be a sunrise unlike any other. The rays of this sun *will* bring healing, but this will come alongside God's judgement. Justice has a price.

The rays of the sun are incredibly powerful. When my car windscreen is frosted over, I try to park where the sun shines on it directly. It's amazing how quickly it clears – I call it 'thermonuclear de-icing'. So imagine the power of the rays of the sun of righteousness. Evil will be destroyed and the earth filled with goodness. What a great hope!

■ PRAYER

What are the injustices in the world which concern you? Pray that the rays of the sun of righteousness will bring healing and restoration.

Romans 13:11b–12 (NIV)

Wake up!

The hour has already come for you to wake up from your slumber, because our salvation is nearer now than when we first believed. The night is nearly over; the day is almost here. So let us put aside the deeds of darkness and put on the armour of light.

'Are we nearly there yet?' Any parent who has been on a long trip with their children will have heard that question. It's one which as Christians we should be thinking about in relation to our salvation. We don't know when that day will dawn – Jesus said that not even he knew that (Matthew 24:36). What is certain is that it will be sooner than before.

It's so easy to live as though the world will carry on like this forever, but it won't. So the challenge is to get ready for the day when Jesus returns, living as though it is already here. If you're going to be ready, what needs to be different? And how should your thinking change? In contrast, think about Jesus and aim to do everything for him and through him. Paul tells us more about the armour of light in Ephesians 6:13–17.

■ PRAYER

Lord Jesus, help me to be awake and ready for that day, whenever it is. Please show me the things in my life I need to change. And as I go through today, help me to see how I can imitate you in everything I do. Amen

Matthew 4:13–14, 16 (NIV)

Light comes to darkness

Leaving Nazareth, [Jesus] went and lived in Capernaum, which was by the lake in the area of Zebulun and Naphtali – to fulfil what was said through the prophet Isaiah: '... The people living in darkness have seen a great light; on those living in the land of the shadow of death a light has dawned.'

What do you think are the dark places in the world? Don't give up hope for them. Often God's light shines in apparently surprising places.

Jesus went to Galilee to start his preaching. It wasn't an obvious place. Cut off from Judea politically, in the past it had been under Assyrian rule, and there was still a large Gentile population. So to start here would mean that later when he went to Jerusalem, he would be virtually a foreigner. But centuries before, this had been prophesied by Isaiah (see verses 15–16), right down to mentioning Zebulun and Naphtali. In this dark place, a great light would shine. Now it *was* shining – the Messiah was there.

This prosperous, fertile area was probably the most densely populated in the Middle East. While it may have been spiritually dark ('the shadow of death'), the light of the world was now among them. Think about the places you know. If Christians are children of the light (Ephesians 5:8), what difference does our presence make?

■ PRAYER
Pray for Christ's light to come to the dark places you know. How could you be an answer to that prayer?

Psalm 130:5–6 (NIV)

Waiting, waiting...

I wait for the Lord, my whole being waits, and in his word I put my hope. I wait for the Lord more than watchmen wait for the morning, more than watchmen wait for the morning.

Sleep is a problem for many. Anxiety, depression, too little exercise, too much caffeine and simply getting older can all affect our sleep patterns. The experience of the watchmen in this psalm, waiting for the morning, is common. It can be so frustrating, can't it? Job puts it brilliantly: 'When I lie down I think, "How long before I get up?" The night drags on, and I toss and turn until dawn' (Job 7:4). It becomes a vicious circle.

This psalm speaks of another kind of waiting. The writer was waiting for God *even more* than for the morning. Perhaps we can turn our waiting for sleep into waiting for God. Some use their time awake to pray for people and needs. But what about simply waiting for God himself? Being still in God's presence can be difficult because of all the distractions around us. But lying in bed with nothing to divert us can be a golden opportunity. You don't have to say anything to God, just recognise that he is there and wait. This kind of prayer 'is not useful or practical. It is simply,' in the words of Henri Nouwen, 'to waste time for and with God'.

■ PRAYER

Lord, help me to wait patiently in your presence at some time today. Amen

Luke 1:77–79 (GW)

New dawn, new day

'You will make his people know that they can be saved through the forgiveness of their sins. A new day will dawn on us from above because our God is loving and merciful. He will give light to those who live in the dark and in death's shadow. He will guide us into the way of peace.'

What's so special about a new day? Isn't every day a new day? Zechariah's extraordinary prophecy here is about a day that will be game-changing. Things will never be the same again. His newborn son John (the Baptist) will prepare the way for the Messiah, and one of his tasks will be to tell the people how they can be saved. Rather than receiving the deliverance from Roman oppression that they are hoping for, they can receive forgiveness for their sins.

What they wanted seemed huge; what they were to receive was so much greater. Deliverance from the Romans was for them only; forgiveness will be on offer to the whole world. This new day will dawn from above. And with it will come a fresh vision of God as loving and merciful, not harsh and judgemental.

I once read J.B. Philips' famous book called *Your God is Too Small*. Like the people of Zechariah's time, might our expectations of God be too low?

■ **PRAYER**

Father God, thank you for the good news of forgiveness of sin. Help me today to both know and share your light and peace. Amen

John 3:19–20 (NIV)

In the shadows

This is the verdict: light has come into the world, but people loved darkness instead of light because their deeds were evil. Everyone who does evil hates the light, and will not come into the light for fear that their deeds will be exposed.

From time to time people go to court to stop a newspaper article being published. Sometimes it's because the story is untrue, but sometimes it's because they don't want the truth to be known. Not everyone likes the light, and dawn is not attractive to everyone. So as the sun rises, some people disappear quickly into the shadows. Not everyone welcomed Jesus when he was on earth, and the same is true now.

Often people reject Jesus because they don't understand who he is or what he can do. But this is not the problem here. Jesus was speaking about people who want to avoid the light because they don't want the truth about themselves to be known.

When I was a child, my dad wrote something in my autograph book about the Bible. He wrote: 'This book will keep you from sin or sin will keep you from this book.' And he was right. There have been times when I've avoided reading the Bible because I didn't want to hear its message. Are we seeking the light or avoiding it?

■ PRAYER

Lord, help me to live in your light today and be ready to face its truth. Amen

Isaiah 60:1–3 (NIV)

Rising sun

'Arise, shine, for your light has come, and the glory of the Lord rises upon you. See, darkness covers the earth and thick darkness is over the peoples, but the Lord rises upon you and his glory appears over you. Nations will come to your light, and kings to the brightness of your dawn.'

The Grand Canyon in the US is spectacular. I visited many years ago, long before the dawn of digital photography, and very quickly used all my film. We rose early while it was still dark so that we could see the sunrise. The first rays of the sun appeared in the gloom and, gradually, the canyon filled with light. The view changed constantly as though a painter was at work, using every colour on the palette and more – it was literally brilliant. And as the sun rose even higher, the light penetrated the recesses and depths of the canyon until everything was visible.

Isaiah's vision of the future is one of great hope – if you can, read the whole chapter to get the full picture. The Lord's glory will rise like the sun, removing every trace of darkness. His light will draw people from all nations and our divisions will be removed. 'He will judge the world with justice and rule the nations with fairness' (Psalm 9:8, NLT). What a great hope!

■ PRAYER

Father of light, I pray that like the rising sun, you will drive away the darkness in our world. Amen

The Gift of Years

 Debbie Thrower is the pioneer of BRF's Anna Chaplaincy for Older People ministry, offering spiritual care to older people, and is widely involved in training and advocacy.

Visit **annachaplaincy.org.uk** to find out more.

Debbie writes...

Welcome! What evocative themes in this issue – song, light, remembrance and angels. I'm reminded of a favourite prayer of an elderly woman who once sent me on a mission: to find this prayer she now has framed in beautiful calligraphy. It's likely to be very old, as the wording is quite tricky to read, but I very much like its message of God listening out through his messenger angels for anyone in need of help, or even the faintest intimation of a person who is 'sorry', however big or small their crime or misdemeanour:

'This Spiritual house Almighty God shall inhabit and hallow it and glorify it and His eye shall be open and His ear intending* on this house night and day; that the asker in it shall receive, the seeker shall find, and they who ring or knock shall enter. Truly every soul converted, penitent of his sin and in this place praying, in heaven graciously shall be heard. The seeker with perfect heart for whatsoever tribulation shall without doubt find help; and to them that come with faithful decisive knock at the door, assistant angels shall open the gates of heaven, receiving and offering to God the prayers of a faithful people.'

So, seek, knock, enter these pages and receive!

Best wishes *Debbie*

* As in the French, and presumably old English, sense of 'entendre', 'to hear'.

The angel project

Sharp-eyed December visitors to Dorchester-on-Thames might have spotted some intriguing little figures half-hidden near the postbox, by the abbey lychgate or close to the school bus stop. These four-inch-high knitted angels, in rainbow colours with outstretched wings, were part of an all-age Advent project at Dorchester Abbey, initiated by resident Denise Line, encouraged by Rector Sue Booys. Denise tells the angels' story:

I got the idea from the social media pages of the church I used to go to in Farnborough, Hampshire. I got in touch with my old friends to find out more, and they told me to contact the organisers of the 'Rushmoor Christmas Angels' project. They, in turn, were very generous with their advice and in 2017 I asked our rector, Sue, if I could have a go at something similar, as part of a major abbey art installation about angels called 'Realms of Glory'.

At first I just put a box in the abbey with some bits and pieces of wool, and then I thought I could do it better, so I made up kits in little plastic bags. In 2019 I made the bags from pages cut from old magazines and made up more elaborate kits with small balls of wool, a pattern and some stuffing for the head of the angel.

The very first angel I got in 2019 was from a young mum, with a two-year-old child. She doesn't live in the village, but she comes to the abbey to worship. She has a floristry business and she's involved in doing the flowers in the abbey, so she's quite a busy person, but nonetheless she was the first person to return a finished angel. And then she got her mother involved, and she's knitted 27 angels!

We very much want it to be an intergenerational project, but it does tend to be the older people who do the actual knitting. It's a lovely thing to do on dark winter evenings – one person I know knits her angels while she's watching the news and finds it very therapeutic. It's much more fun than knitting squares for blankets, and the variety and creativity in the finished angels is amazing. Sometimes I finish them off, stitching them up and maybe adding faces or hair, and we attach a label giving details of all the abbey services for Advent, Christmas and Epiphany, and also a tiny star to tie in the Angel Project with the Church of England 'Follow the Star' initiative. Then at the main Advent Sunday service the angels are taken forward and blessed, and after the service the congregation gets a chance to see them all before they're hidden around the village.

Over the next few days, I see how many angels I've got, and work out which days I'll go out on which route – I work with a map of the village so they're well distributed. I've been told that some families go out on special angel hunts, and I know that some people in the village have long walks to school and look for the angels along the way.

I only have one bugbear about this, and that's when people think this is a project for the children. It's not – it's for absolutely everyone. I know of one very elderly person who found an angel on her doorstep and it meant the world to her. It's a symbolic thing, and the angel project is for everyone.

Even if people don't have a church background, they seem to respond to idea of angels. Images of angels are so popular even in the secular world, as we found with 'Realms of Glory'.

Angels have been important to me personally. At a practical level, I just love making things and I find any excuse to make something. But more than that, I went to school in Oxford and our school hymn was 'Lead, kindly light' because the school was in Littlemore, which is where John Henry Newman was based for some of his remarkable life. I've always loved the hymn – though it must be sung to 'Alberta', nothing else – and the final words have always meant a lot to me: 'And with the morn those angel faces smile, which I have loved long since, and lost awhile.'

My hope and dream for these angels this Advent is that when people find an angel, whether they're looking for one or not, it will bring them joy; I hope that it may bring them comfort, if that's what they need, and that it will remind them how the angels feature so strongly in the Christmas story. I hope it might encourage some people who haven't been before, or haven't been for a long time, to come and join the congregation here in the abbey during Advent and Christmas. But what I really hope is that people will find the joy of the angels.

Denise Line talked about how, since her school days, she'd been inspired by the words of John Henry Newman's much-loved, often-sung hymn 'Lead, kindly light'. Originally written as a poem, 'The pillar of cloud', at a time of great anguish in the new saint's life, these verses echo with all our themes: light, remembrance and angels.

Lead, kindly light

Lead, kindly light, amid the encircling gloom,
lead thou me on;
the night is dark, and I am far from home;
lead thou me on.
Keep thou my feet; I do not ask to see
the distant scene; one step enough for me.

I was not ever thus, nor prayed that thou
shouldst lead me on;
I loved to choose and see my path; but now
lead thou me on.
I loved the garish day, and, spite of fears,
pride ruled my will: remember not past years.

So long thy power hath blest me, sure it still
will lead me on,
o'er moor and fen, o'er crag and torrent, till
the night is gone,
and with the morn those angel faces smile,
which I have loved long since, and lost awhile.

John Henry Newman (1801–90)

And staying with the theme of angels – God's messengers – here's a delightful and thought-provoking retelling of the shepherds' story. The shepherds are reimagined as security guards watching over a building by night. It's from the BRF ideas hub: **ideas.brf.org.uk**.

A shudder of angels

Watching over their flocks… of screens by night,
the security guards monitored the lonely hours
in the high-rise office blocks, not far from Bethlehem.
But there was nothing to report.
No break-in; no break-out.
All was safe.

Night-watchman work is a strange occupation –
no skill required other than to stay awake while others sleep;
to keep alert and guard against the unexpected.
It's an unattractive job with antisocial hours,
serving the great financial houses
that feed the temples of Mammon.

And so they watched, on duty, in silence and in solitude,
while digital images flickered, the CCTV jumped channels
and eyelids drooped,
as black-and-white movie stars from yesteryear came out
to grace the TV screen.
But there was nothing to report.
No break-in; no break-out.
All was safe.

Until that night – the night that changed everything –
when suddenly the electric sparked, lights flashed,
the pictures danced and grew bright with strangeness;

when every screen faltered, froze
and then faded into a dazzling brightness.
Was this a break-in or a break-out?
Something was happening.
There was something to report.

Alarm bells rang inside the watchmen's heads
but they couldn't move,
entranced by what they saw. For, lo,
a great shudder of angels appeared in each and every monitor,
a fearful sight that told them not to be afraid.
'Something glorious has happened,' they said;
but not up in the luxury penthouse suites above,
nor within the vast executive board rooms below,
nor yet in the open-plan office spaces elsewhere in the building;
but in the basement,
among the dirt and debris, swept out of sight.

Something had come to overturn from underneath
the well-oiled machines of human commerce;
to redistribute wealth and wisdom and wonder,
and reconcile accounts for all.
They should go. Now. Abandon their soulless work.
Go and discover the new thing,
wrapped in strips of computer packaging
and lying in a cardboard box.

So they broke out and found the one who had broken in –
an intruder bathed in neon from the streetlamp outside.
And it was just as they had been told.
Without identity badge or appointment,
he had bypassed all the normal protocols
and was in the building,
undoing their security and ours.

As one day he would go on to unbalance the old statements,
turn profits into losses
and re-audit the transactions of all our lives.
Now this was something to report.
A break-in, and a break-out.
Something had happened.
And from now on the world's security would never be safe again.

Remember, remember

David Butterfield

'Remember, remember the fifth of November' – so begins a well-known rhyme in the UK associated with Bonfire Night. Perhaps you, like me, have clear memories of that night from your early childhood.

Some memories are precious and some are painful. As we get older, we can find that our short-term memories do not work as well as they used to. Last Christmas, I agreed to accompany some carol singing on the piano at a local care home. On the day I totally forgot about it, and as a result I was extremely embarrassed. In contrast, some of our childhood memories, like those of Bonfire Night, can be as vivid as the day they occurred.

In this series we're going to reflect on some of the 260+ instances in the Bible when the word 'remember' is found. Sometimes they will be about God remembering something – or not remembering. Sometimes they will be about our remembering.

As we focus on these, my prayer is that you will be encouraged by the way that God remembers his people, and that it will help you to remember things about God that will deepen your walk with him.

As I searched the scriptures for references to 'remembering', I found this promise: 'The righteous will never be moved; they will be remembered forever' (Psalm 112:6, NRSV). May we always remember this truth.

1 Samuel 1:19b–20a (NRSV)

God remembers Hannah

The Lord remembered [Hannah]. In due time Hannah conceived and bore a son. She named him Samuel.

Once, when I was serving on the staff of York Minster, I picked up a bundle of prayer request cards that visitors had filled in that day and selected four to pray for at Evensong. One of them was from a couple asking God to enable them to become parents and, unbeknown to me, they were present in the service. Immediately afterwards, they came up to me and thanked me for choosing to pray for them. I found myself spontaneously saying the words that High Priest Eli said to Hannah, 'May the God of Israel grant what you have asked of him' (v. 17, NIV).

I don't know whether God 'remembered' this couple, but in the first book of Samuel we are told that 'the Lord remembered' Hannah, and as a result Samuel was born. Similarly, in the book of Genesis we're told that 'God remembered Rachel' (Genesis 30:22), who also longed for a child.

Have you been praying for a particular thing for a very long time? May the stories of Hannah and Rachel encourage you to keep praying.

■ **PRAYER**

Heavenly Father, as you remembered Hannah, please remember those today who have prayed for something for a long time. Amen

Psalm 77:11–12 (NRSV)

Choosing to remember

I will call to mind the deeds of the Lord; I will remember your wonders of old. I will meditate on all your work, and muse on your mighty deeds.

Not long ago I lost my credit card. I was fairly certain I had just put it down somewhere, but I couldn't remember where. Although I searched, I couldn't find it. Then a few hours later, when my mind was completely absorbed in something else, out of the blue I suddenly remembered that I had changed my shirt and that my card was probably in the first shirt's pocket. It was.

Many of our memories are like that – passive, beyond our control, rising to the surface when we're focused on something else. By contrast, the writer of Psalm 77 tells how he deliberately chooses to remember the wonderful things God has done in the past.

Remembering is something we can do as an act of the will, as a habit, as a discipline. I sometimes spend a few moments looking back and remembering an occasion when God acted in a special way in my life, and I encourage you to do the same. Reflect on the circumstances of that time and how you felt when God touched your life.

May that encourage you in your life of faith today.

■ **PRAYER**

Heavenly Father, thank you for the times when you have intervened in my life and brought me blessing. Remind me of these blessings every day. Amen

Judges 8:33–34 (NRSV, abridged)

Forgetting to remember

As soon as Gideon died, the Israelites relapsed and... did not remember the Lord their God, who had rescued them from the hand of all their enemies on every side.

The circumstances of my life changed in 1970 when I went from Yorkshire to Surrey, to Royal Holloway College to study for a music degree. I had been a churchgoer from my Sunday school days, but the change and freedom of university meant that I didn't actively 'remember the Lord'. (I was to come to a full faith two years later – but that's another story.)

When circumstances changed for the people of Israel, we are told that they 'did not remember the Lord their God'. In their case, it was Gideon who had been their inspiration, and without his strong lead, they regressed spiritually. In my case, it was attending my local church before university that had kept me 'remembering' the Lord and on the right track.

As we look back over our lives, we may be able to think of some occasions when our circumstances changed and as a result we did not remember the Lord in the way we had before. Or there may have been a more recent occasion when our circumstances changed – perhaps when someone who was a strong support to us spiritually died or moved away – which caused us not to remember God as we used to.

Being aware of this can be a first step towards remembering the Lord again and drawing near to him once more.

■ PRAYER

Heavenly Father, help me to remember you, even when those who have supported me are no longer close by. Amen

Jonah 2:7a, 9b (NRSV)

Out of the depths

'As my life was ebbing away, I remembered the Lord; and my prayer came to you… Deliverance belongs to the Lord!'

The story of Jonah is well known – how he tried to run away from God and ended up being swallowed by a big fish, often referred to as a whale. Afterwards, he described his distressful situation with graphic imagery: 'The waters closed in over me; the deep surrounded me; weeds were wrapped around my head' (v. 5). It was at that point that he remembered the Lord.

There are two ways we can react to God when we go through tough times. One is to doubt him, draw back from him and blame him for what is happening to us. The other is to turn to him more earnestly. In 1940, the author and theologian C.S. Lewis wrote a book called *The Problem of Pain*. In it he writes, 'God whispers to us in our pleasures… but shouts in our pains: it is his megaphone to rouse a deaf world.' If we remember the Lord in times of difficulty, we might find that we hear his voice more clearly and sense his presence more closely.

So as we think of how Jonah remembered the Lord when he was going through his dreadful experience, may we learn from him and do likewise.

■ PRAYER

Heavenly Father, help those who are going through difficult times to remember you today. Amen

Jeremiah 31:34b (NRSV)

Remember no more

I will forgive their iniquity, and remember their sin no more.

When an issue occurs between two people, it's always a relief when one of them says, 'Let's forget all about it.' As a result, the friendship is restored and we can feel a huge sense of relief. It can be hard to do, but it is actually possible for us to choose to forget something.

This is also true with God. In one of his prophecies, Jeremiah pointed to the time when God would establish a new relationship with his people, write his law on our hearts and remember our sins no more. This prophecy was fulfilled through the life, death and resurrection of Jesus. Because of what he did for us, God deliberately chooses to forget our sins.

I wonder how much we take this on board – that when we confess our sins, that is the end of them. When we get older, some of our misdemeanours from many years ago can sometimes surface in our minds. Perhaps that's why David once prayed, 'Do not remember the sins of my youth' (Psalm 25:7).

If you find that your conscience is sometimes pricked because of something wrong you did in the past, allow the truth of God's promise that he will remember our sin no more to penetrate deep into your inner self.

■ PRAYER

Heavenly Father, thank you that when we confess our sins, you will forgive us and remember our sins no more. Amen

Hebrews 13:3 (NIV)

Thinking of you

Continue to remember those in prison as if you were together with them in prison, and those who are ill-treated as if you yourselves were suffering.

Have you ever received a card from a friend with the message, 'Thinking of you'? Such a message can come as a great encouragement in tough times.

The writer of the letter to the Hebrews encourages his readers to remember those in prison and those who are being mistreated. From what we know of the context in which the letter was written, it's likely that he was thinking of their fellow Christians who were being persecuted for their faith. By 'remember', he was probably urging his readers to care for them in practical ways and to pray for them.

Today, there must be hundreds of thousands of people who are wrongly imprisoned and mistreated. In Hebrews, we are encouraged to think ourselves into their situations, because that will motivate us to help them in any way we can: practically, financially and, importantly, by praying for them.

■ PRAYER

Heavenly Father, I pray for prisoners of conscience around the world and for those wrongly imprisoned and mistreated. Please strengthen them and bring them justice and freedom. Amen

Numbers 11:5–6 (NRSV)

Fish and cucumbers

'We remember the fish we used to eat in Egypt for nothing, the cucumbers, the melons, the leeks, the onions, and the garlic; but now our strength is dried up, and there is nothing at all but this manna to look at.'

Today's scripture reference is from when the people of Israel were in the desert and God fed them miraculously with a special food called manna. But they were far from happy with the manna and, in their memories, they harked back to the 'wonderful' days in Egypt when they used to have haddock and salad for tea. They failed to remember their cruel slavery. God was not impressed with their grumbling.

When we're older and look back, we can easily think of the many things that are different today and wish that we could return to how things were. But, of course, we cannot go back to a rose-tinted past, and the problem with this sort of wistful remembering is that it leads to negative thoughts and feelings within.

One antidote is to remember to thank God for the things that make life good for us *today* and, as the old hymn puts it, to 'count our blessings and name them one by one'.*

■ PRAYER

Heavenly Father, thank you for the many blessings, spiritual and material, that you lavish on me each day. Amen

* 'Count your blessings' by Johnson Oatman Jr (1856–1926).

Exodus 20:8 (NRSV)

A day to remember

Remember the sabbath day, and keep it holy.

My father owned a small business manufacturing watch glasses in Bradford in West Yorkshire. I recall one Sunday that he needed to get something from his work, and I went with him in the car. I remember being amazed at how the city was completely deserted compared with the usual hustle and bustle. Sunday trading has certainly changed our Sundays out of all recognition.

The fourth commandment directs us to 'remember' the sabbath day. For me as a child, that meant a list of things I was not allowed to do, and my memories are of restricted, boring Sundays. I don't think that was God's intention. I believe his idea was for it to be a special day when we can rest from work, spend time with family and friends and focus on our relationship with God.

So could we make Sunday the most special day of the week? Perhaps it could be the day to pick up the phone and have a conversation with friends and family, or the day to invite someone to come and see us. It could be the day when we allow ourselves a special treat of some sort.

Sunday is also a day when we can choose to give God more of our time than on other days. The author of the letter to the Hebrews uses the word 'rest' to describe the blessing of knowing God through Jesus. In a quiet moment, we could close our eyes and ask the Holy Spirit to make that sense of sabbath rest real to us.

■ PRAYER

Heavenly Father, show me how I can make Sunday the best day of the week. Amen

Luke 22:19 (NRSV)

Remembering Jesus

Then [Jesus] took a loaf of bread, and when he had given thanks, he broke it and gave it to [his disciples], saying, 'This is my body, which is given for you. Do this in remembrance of me.'

When our two children were small and we lived in Shropshire, I took them on an outing to the Severn Valley Railway. I recall crossing a footbridge as a steam engine was leaving the station, and we were engulfed in a cloud of steam and smoke. It has such a distinctive smell, and in a flash I found myself transported back to when I used to go trainspotting at the age of eleven. All our five senses can trigger different memories in an amazing way, but none more powerfully than our sense of smell.

When Jesus told us how to remember him, he chose a way that would bombard our senses: we hear the words of scripture spoken; we see, smell and taste the bread and the wine; and we touch the bread and the cup. Christians believe that when we receive these tokens of Christ's death, we receive the spiritual blessings that Christ won for us when he died.

So taking Communion isn't just about remembering Jesus in the same way that we might remember someone else who has died. Through remembering Jesus in this way, we strengthen our faith and deepen our relationship with him.

■ PRAYER

Lord Jesus Christ, thank you that you left us this simple meal as a way of remembering you with all our senses. Thank you for the blessings of forgiveness and eternal life. Amen

Philippians 1:3–4 (NRSV)

Fond memories

I thank my God every time I remember you, constantly praying with joy in every one of my prayers for all of you.

As you look back over your life, what are some of your fondest memories? I imagine that some of your most precious memories will be of particular people and the occasions you spent with them.

When Paul wrote to the Christians who lived in Philippi, he recounted with great joy and affection his memory of being with them. He had clearly been blessed by the love and support they gave him, especially when he was in prison. These were indeed fond and precious memories.

If you cast your mind back and remember some of your fondest memories, which people come to mind? If you were to jot down their names, you might be surprised by the length of the list. Some of them may have died; others you may still see regularly. So why not make a list and then spend some time working down it, remembering each individual one by one and recalling these treasured memories? Like Paul, thank God for each one, for the love you received and for all the many ways these special relationships have enriched your life.

■ PRAYER
Heavenly Father, thank you for all those people who through my life have shown great love to me and given me support and encouragement. Amen

God's messengers

Angela Tilby

As we grow older, we become more aware of how the choices we have made earlier in our lives have shaped us. This can be a source of pride or regret. But whatever we have done with our lives so far, we should never think of ourselves as autonomous beings. We exist with and for others.

This is obvious when we think of those relationships that have sustained us and to which we ourselves contribute. What we are often less aware of is the hidden dimension of our choices, our constant interaction with God. The Bible is rich in references to the angels, God's messengers. They interact with human beings at the critical points in their lives, bringing warning, offering comfort and opening up new vocations. They are part of the unseen company of heaven, reminding us that God's creativity is not limited to what we see.

God is the creator of all things 'visible and invisible', as the creed puts it. Religious belief may be declining in our time, but, curiously, belief in angels is remarkably resilient. For some, they are a stepping stone to faith, evidence that there are indeed 'more things in heaven and earth'* than our current philosophies of life find it easy to imagine.

* *Hamlet* by William Shakespeare, Act I, Scene V.

Genesis 18:1–3 (NRSV)

Entertaining angels

The Lord appeared to Abraham by the oaks of Mamre, as he sat at the entrance of his tent in the heat of the day. He looked up and saw three men standing near him. When he saw them, he ran from the tent entrance to meet them, and bowed down to the ground. He said, 'My lord, if I find favour with you, do not pass by your servant.'

The appearance of the three men to Abraham is one of the most important hinges in the biblical story, because the visitors come to announce the birth of the son and heir promised by God. Abraham and Sarah were not to end their days in frustration, in spite of Sarah's childlessness.

Abraham's humble recognition of the heavenly visitors shows that he had not lost his memory of God's promise, or his desire to see its fulfilment. There is a challenge here for us. Angels come from the future, and they disturb any tendency we might have to dwell in the past. We need to keep our hearts ready and expectant, open to God's grace, whatever our circumstances in the here and now.

■ **PRAYER**

Lord God, we greet you as we look for your coming to us today. Give us grace to see you in those we meet and to be faithful to all your promises. Give us insight to respond to what is unexpected and to receive your guidance with humble and thankful hearts. Amen

Exodus 14:19–20 (NRSV)

The pillar of cloud

The angel of God who was going before the Israelite army moved and went behind them; and the pillar of cloud moved from in front of them and took its place behind them. It came between the army of Egypt and the army of Israel. And so the cloud was there with the darkness, and it lit up the night; one did not come near the other all night.

As Emlyn Williams reflected earlier, the night can be a difficult time, especially when we sense frailty in ourselves and those we love. Sleepless nights can be very long, and we are perhaps most vulnerable to anxiety in those dark hours just before dawn. Yet the night is also a time of mystery, revelation and transition.

God is as present at night as in the day, and his saving acts often occur in the dark. For the Israelites, the terrifying night they spent at the edge of the Red Sea was the time of their divine deliverance from slavery. The angel and the protective cloud which had guided them on their journey moved to come between them and their enemies. This kept them safe while God drove back the sea, making a path to freedom.

■ PRAYER

Lord, the darkness is not dark to you; the night is as bright as the day. Lighten our dark days and our troubling nights by your protective presence, and in your mercy may we trust in you and so come to know our true freedom. Amen

Isaiah 6:1–3 (NRSV)

Realms of glory

In the year that King Uzziah died, I saw the Lord sitting on a throne, high and lofty; and the hem of his robe filled the temple. Seraphs were in attendance above him; each had six wings: with two they covered their faces, and with two they covered their feet, and with two they flew. And one called to another and said, 'Holy, holy, holy is the Lord of hosts; the whole earth is full of his glory.'

While the prophet Isaiah is worshipping in the temple in Jerusalem, he has a vision of the heavenly temple. The Lord sits enthroned on high, surrounded by winged and worshipping angels. The Hebrew word for 'holy' implies separation. God is unlike us, utterly other. The prophet is privileged to look at mysteries humans cannot normally see.

We may find public worship a mixed experience; familiarity and distraction can make it difficult to keep focused. But Isaiah's vision alerts us to the unseen world beyond us. God's glory is at the horizons of our vision, the glory which fills the whole earth, surrounding us whether we are aware of it or not.

■ PRAYER

Holy God, lift our hearts up to you and show us a glint of your glory this day. May the knowledge of your presence, in and through all things, be a lamp to our feet and a light on our way, that we may come to this day's end in peace, having seen your salvation. Amen

Isaiah 6:6–8 (NRSV)

Holy, holy, holy...

Then one of the seraphs flew to me, holding a live coal that had been taken from the altar with a pair of tongs. The seraph touched my mouth with it and said: 'Now that this has touched your lips, your guilt has been departed and your sin is blotted out.' Then I heard the voice of the Lord saying, 'Whom shall I send, and who will go for us?' And I said, 'Here am I; send me.'

It is a truth we often do not wish to receive that there is no growth, either in body or spirit, without change and sometimes pain. In the spiritual life, complacency is death. Only by disciplined honesty do we become free enough to serve God with the whole of ourselves.

The prophet's lips need to be seared, his speech purged; only then will he be free to respond to God's call. Life is full of trials and transitions, some of which may be deeply painful. Yet, often out of these times of anguish a new call emerges. The angel who brings the burning coal to our lips is sent not only to make us whole but to equip us for the service which is also perfect freedom.

■ **PRAYER**

Lord, send your angel with the fire of deliverance, purge our complaints and our complaining, our bitterness and our murmurings against others. Set us free, once again, to respond to your love. Amen

Daniel 10:10–12 (NRSV)

'Fear not,' said he...

But then a hand touched me and roused me to my hands and knees. He said to me, 'Daniel, greatly beloved, pay attention to the words that I am going to speak to you. Stand on your feet, for I have now been sent to you.' So while he was speaking this word to me, I stood up trembling. He said to me, 'Do not fear, Daniel, for from the first day that you set your mind to gain understanding and to humble yourself before your God, your words have been heard, and I have come because of your words.'

When we are overwhelmed with fear or anxiety, it is difficult to hold on to the fact that we are loved by God. Daniel sees catastrophe lying ahead for his people and is physically and mentally overwhelmed by fear of the future. Yet the angel that comes to him comes with reassurance.

The human condition is one of frailty. We cannot always be strong or resilient, and though we can be frustrated at our own limitations, they do not hinder the work of God. Daniel remains God's 'greatly beloved', and so are we. All that is asked of us is faith.

■ PRAYER

Lord, send your angel of consolation to all who despair of the future and see no hope in themselves. Help us to know that we are greatly beloved and that today, tomorrow and forever, the future is in your hands. Amen

Luke 1:26–30 (NRSV)

Annunciation

In the sixth month the angel Gabriel was sent by God to a town in Galilee called Nazareth, to a virgin betrothed to a man whose name was Joseph, of the house of David. The virgin's name was Mary. And he came to her and said, 'Greetings, favoured one! The Lord is with you.' But she was much perplexed by his words and pondered what sort of greeting this might be. The angel said to her, 'Do not be afraid, Mary, for you have found favour with God.'

These words are so familiar from the Christmas story that we might wonder what they have to say specifically to us. But the point here is that angels are rarely expected. We do not see them coming. Their arrival is a surprise and their message is at first perplexing.

Our human imagination is limited to what we know, hope for or fear, and when the unexpected happens our most basic response is likely to be fear. Yet God looks on Mary with favour. In her, he shows his goodwill towards us all. He desires good things for us, for the human race and for all creation. Today, we can rest confidently in that promise.

■ **PRAYER**

Lord, you surprise us with your greeting and call us to attend to your promises. Give us the confidence and trust to say with blessed Mary, 'Behold the handmaid of the Lord; be it unto me according to thy word' (Luke 1:38, KJV). Amen

Mark 1:9–13 (NRSV)

Ministering angels

In those days Jesus came from Nazareth of Galilee and was baptised by John in the Jordan. And just as he was coming up out of the water, he saw the heavens torn apart and the Spirit descending like a dove on him. And a voice came from heaven, 'You are my Son, the Beloved; with you I am well pleased.' And the Spirit immediately drove him out into the wilderness. He was in the wilderness for forty days, tempted by Satan; and he was with the wild beasts; and the angels waited on him.

Mark's gospel shows us Jesus experiencing the extremes of life: both blessing and severe testing. The blessing comes first. He knows that he is God's beloved Son. So with us, our baptism binds us into a fellowship with Jesus which no trial or adversity can destroy. But assurance is followed by temptation. Jesus is driven out into a place of isolation, danger and temptation.

Like us, he wonders about whether he really is God's Son and whether his future really is in God's hands. Like us, he is tempted to give in to the seductive voice of despair. Being 'with' the wild beasts, he experiences passivity and helplessness. But even at this point, the angels are on his side. It is their silent ministry that upholds us today, whatever today brings.

■ PRAYER

Lord, give us grace to follow in your steps. And send your holy angels to protect, console and finally deliver us from all evil. Amen

Matthew 28:1–2 (NRSV)

Resurrection angel

After the sabbath, as the first day of the week was dawning, Mary Magdalene and the other Mary went to see the tomb. And suddenly there was a great earthquake; for an angel of the Lord, descending from heaven, came and rolled back the stone and sat on it.

The resurrection of Jesus is the core of the gospel. It is the unexpected announcement that death is not the last word in the drama of human life. Seen from God's perspective, the end of human life heralds the glory of heaven. The resurrection angel stands in the void of unknowing between the sad expectation of the two Marys and God's heavenly vindication of his Son.

No wonder, in Matthew's version, the arrival of the angel is announced by an earthquake. Fragile human beings are made of earth, with all too earthly hopes and fears. But we are made *for* heaven. Our limited minds can barely cope with the notion of heaven, and our experience seems to show that life is often more tragic than triumphant. But the Easter angel waits to descend into our lives, to bring us the good news from heaven: 'Christ is risen.'

■ **PRAYER**

Lord, we are creatures of dust and to dust we shall return. As we grieve for all that has gone wrong in our lives, we turn to you in confidence that you can and will restore, revive and remake us, after the pattern of your risen Son, Jesus Christ our Lord. Amen

Matthew 28:5–7 (NRSV)

'My message for you'

But the angel said to the women, 'Do not be afraid. I know that you are looking for Jesus who was crucified. He is not here; for he has been raised, as he said. Come, see the place where he lay. Then go quickly and tell his disciples, "He has been raised from the dead, and indeed he is going ahead of you to Galilee; there you will see him." This is my message for you.'

The angel of the resurrection comes with news from the future. Jesus has gone ahead into Galilee and is waiting for his disciples to catch up with him. In later life, we may often find ourselves dwelling on the past. There can be a purpose to this if it opens up for us dimensions of God's love that we had missed at the time.

The past is always fruitful if it is linked to the future. But if it is not, it becomes a dead end, full of fruitless regret. Jesus goes to Galilee to renew his call to his disciples. As we recall our younger lives, we may be able to respond to God at a deeper and more knowing level than we were able to at the time. He raises us not to our old lives, but to a new life in Christ. Do not be afraid.

■ PRAYER

Lord, as we commit our past to you, so raise us to new life with you, forever. Amen

Revelation 14:6–7 (NRSV)

To God be the glory

Then I saw another angel flying in mid-heaven, with an eternal gospel to proclaim to those who live on the earth – to every nation and tribe and language and people. He said in a loud voice, 'Fear God and give him glory, for the hour of his judgement has come; and worship him who made heaven and earth, the sea and the springs of water.'

Angels are God's messengers. In the imagery of the Bible, they travel between earth and heaven. They come from the future and show us where God's purpose lies, both for individuals and for the whole human race. The eternal gospel is an invitation to all humanity to live with reverence towards God. God is worthy of our worship because he is the source of all that is. We are utterly dependent on him from our first cry to our last breath.

A fulfilled life is one that is shaped by worship, gratitude and dependence on God. Much of our contemporary culture is shaped by the belief that we are alone in the universe; that we should chart our own destiny according to our own whims and impulses. But we are not alone. We are surrounded all the time by messengers of God's love, encouraging, surprising and guiding us. The gospel is eternal.

■ **PRAYER**

Lord, teach us fear of you, which is wisdom, and love of you, which is true life, and make us messengers of your joy. Amen

Giving for the future

Eliashib the high priest and his fellow priests went to work and rebuilt the Sheep Gate. They dedicated it and set its doors in place, building as far as the Tower of the Hundred, which they dedicated, and as far as the Tower of Hananel. The men of Jericho built the adjoining section, and Zakkur son of Imri built next to them.

Nehemiah 3:1–2 (NIV)

The 32 verses of Nehemiah 3 recount the story of the rebuilding of the walls of Jerusalem. A whole host of names follow in quick succession – perhaps not the Bible passage I would like to be asked to read aloud at the front of church for fear of mispronunciation.

Yet this chapter is one of my firm favourites from the whole of the Bible and one that I return to frequently.

The Bible affirms that each person is important, made in the image of God, and each person in the church has a part to play. The different parts come together to make the whole, and they cannot function without each other.

I know of many who at times have felt overstretched or under-appreciated in their work and ministry – perhaps feeling that no one notices. Nehemiah 3 reminds us that every stone laid, every timber cut and every work undertaken is seen by God, and he knows his workers by name.

Throughout BRF's story, our ministry has grown beyond our expectation, thanks to those who have given generously, prayed faithfully and served tirelessly without seeking recognition.

They – and you – are known by God. Thank you. Could you help support this work?

For further information about making a gift to BRF
in your will, please visit **brf.org.uk/lastingdifference**,
contact **+44 (0)1235 462305** or email **giving@brf.org.uk**.

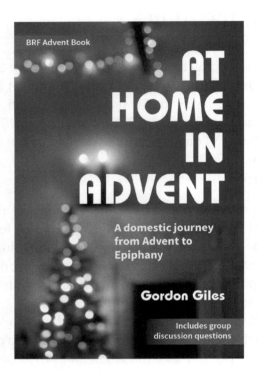

Focusing on a range of everyday objects, some obviously festive, others less so, Gordon Giles reflects on their spiritual significance, meaning and message in today's world. Each chapter consists of a Bible passage, reflection and a concluding prayer, and discussion questions for groups are also included. Beginning with chapters on journeying and travel, the book moves though major Advent themes of expectation, waiting, mortality and hope to the joy of incarnation and salvation.

At Home in Advent
A domestic journey from Advent to Epiphany
Gordon Giles
978 0 85746 980 9 £8.99
brfonline.org.uk

Using the metaphor of pilgrimage, Sally Welch walks alongside us as leader and guide, but also fellow traveller, to explore how we can understand this biblical principle and make it our own. This book is divided into sections of a journey, beginning with the preparations necessary before setting out, exploring the obstacles which might be put in our path and sharing ways in which the journey can be made easier and more productive.

Journey to Contentment
Pilgrimage principles for everyday life
Sally Welch
978 0 85746 326 5 £8.99
brfonline.org.uk

To order

Online: **brfonline.org.uk**
Telephone: +44 (0)1865 319700
Mon–Fri 9.15–17.30
Post: complete this form and send to the address below

Delivery times within the UK are normally 15 working days. Prices are correct at the time of going to press but may change without prior notice.

Title	Issue*	Price	Qty	Total
At Home in Advent		£8.99		
Journey to Contentment		£8.99		
Bible Reflections for Older People (single copy)	Jan/May* 21	£5.15		

delete as appropriate

POSTAGE AND PACKING CHARGES			
Order value	UK	Europe	Rest of world
Under £7.00	£2.00		
£7.00–£29.99	£3.00	Available on request	Available on request
£30.00 and over	FREE		

Total value of books	
Postage and packing	
Total for this order	

Please complete in BLOCK CAPITALS

Title .... First name/initials .... Surname ....

Address ....

.... Postcode ....

Acc. No. .... Telephone ....

Email ....

Method of payment

☐ Cheque (made payable to BRF) ☐ MasterCard / Visa

Card no. ☐☐☐☐ ☐☐☐☐ ☐☐☐☐ ☐☐☐☐

Expires end [M M] [Y Y]   Security code* ☐☐☐   Last 3 digits on the reverse of the card

Signature* .... Date .... / .... / ....

*ESSENTIAL IN ORDER TO PROCESS YOUR ORDER

Please return this form to:
BRF, 15 The Chambers, Vineyard, Abingdon OX14 3FE | enquiries@brf.org.uk
To read our terms and conditions, please visit **brfonline.org.uk/terms**.

The Bible Reading Fellowship (BRF) is a Registered Charity (233280)